THE NEW LIFE IN CHRIST JESUS

To My Wife

Who has been my untiring helper in whatever I have said or written for thirty-one blessed years. Always abiding in the ministries of a Christian home, she has left to me the thanks and prayers of those who have been blessed through our joint labours, content so only that Christ was exalted.

To the Reader

All of the matter composing this book was preached to my congregations in my two pastorates at Dallas, Texas, and Northfield, Massachusetts, and all, save the address on "The Imparted Life," were published first in the "Dallas News." These, re-printed in "The Christian Worker's Magazine," awoke a desire which seemed to be unusually widespread that these teachings concerning the New Life in Christ Jesus might be collected into a book. This, by arrangement with The Bible Institute Colportage Association, has now been done.

The book is here and now committed to the care of Him whom it seeks to exalt in the fervent prayer that through His grace it may show the way into happy, victorious, fruitful Christian living to many in bondage.

C. I. SCOFIELD

Greyshingles
Douglaston, N. Y.
April, 1915.

Contents

I

The Inner Life

Text: "I have heard of thee by the hearing of the ear, but now mine eye seeth thee: wherefore I abhor myself."—Job 42:5, 6.

SOMEONE has called the Book of Job "The Epic of the Inner Life." It is most felicitous. We all know that there is an inner life; that within the barriers of our being, behind all activities and externalities, we ourselves live. We all know that there is transacted the real life. We all know that there we are solitary, that there every man is a hermit.

And while this, past all controversy, is true, in another sense this strange inner life is immensely populous. Passions, desires, temptations, lurid and demoniacal thoughts, angelic thoughts, prayers, adorations, mean selfishnesses, wrestle and plead, and it is into this chaos that faith brings the nature of God, and the life of the risen Christ, and the immense peace and power and joy of the Holy Spirit's

11

indwelling. And we all know that when we have received eternal life we have written but the first chapter in the new history of the inner life. New conflicts, new victories, alas! new defeats, too.

The most commonplace Christian whom you know is transacting in the recesses of his being an epic.

And we know that this inner life is, finally, the source and spring of the outer life. It is, of course, possible to keep these dissimilar for years, but soon or late the inner life becomes determinative of the external life. It is with this life, therefore, that God most concerns Himself. It is the distinctive characteristic of the gospel dispensation. "Now is the ax laid to the root of the tree," says the forerunner, John. "Make the tree good, and his fruit good," is almost the opening word of Christ. It was always so, indeed. "Behold, thou desirest truth in the inward parts." "The Lord pondereth the heart."

I can not, I think, do better than to take the last chapter of the Book of Job for my point of departure, verses 5 and 6:

"I have heard of thee by the hearing of the ear, but now mine eye seeth thee; wherefore I abhor myself, and repent in dust and ashes." It is

THE CRISIS OF THE TROUBLED PATRIARCH

The thing itself is very simple. "I have heard of thee by the hearing of the ear." There was a testimony concerning God which had come to Job, and upon which he had based a true faith and a good life. Ordinarily, Christian experience has just that history. There is a record concerning Christ, His person and work. It is God's testimony, and we receive it and set to our seal that God is true. We are saved. It is a very real faith, though a faith based wholly upon testimony, the hearing of the ear. That was the faith of Job down to the very last chapter.

Here was a godly man whose outward life was so blameless that God could challenge the malice of Satan himself to find a flaw in it. Nor was he but negatively good. He was a good man in the positive sense. His life counted on the right and helpful side of things.

Then began that strange dealing of God, that permitted chastening, which has been the mystery in so many other lives. How strange a thing that the best man of his time should be the most troubled; should be the man upon whom, as it seemed, the hand of God lay most heavily. And the fact, as you know, called out various interpretations. The opinion of Satan concerning this man's goodness and usefulness was that he was a mere hireling. "Hast not thou made an hedge about him?" You have given him unusual prosperity, and in a certain sense you have bribed him. That was Satan's opinion. That was a lie. And God permitted Satan to demonstrate the falsity of his theory of this man's life. God said, in effect, "Take away the hedge"; and then you know what happened: his property went, his children went, and yet the integrity of the man remained. He did not curse God. And then Satan fell back upon another theory which was just as false as the other. He said: "Skin for skin; yea, all that a man hath will he give for his life." You have left the man his health. "Put forth now thine hand, and touch his bone and his flesh, and he will curse thee to thy face." And so that was permitted. His health went, grievous pains fell upon him. Bereft of property, bereft of family, bereft of health, and yet this man, with a faith which was founded upon a hearing about God, maintained his integrity.

And then came the theories of his friends. They agreed in the belief that there must be in his life some secret sin, although he had succeeded in covering it from human vision. They were very sure that the only explanation of the sorrows which were falling so heavily upon him was, that he was a hypocrite; was not as good as he seemed to be, and upon that belief they argued the question with him. But Job knew that also to be false, and he made good his contention that he was not a hypocrite.

A VISION OF GOD

And now we come to the real epic of his inner life. God Himself took up the matter. And if you follow the closing chapters of this wonderful Book of Job, you will find the whole mechanics, so to speak, of the deeper dealing of God with the inner life of a saint whom He is about to make saintly.

There was, first of all, the unveiling of His power, His majesty, His greatness.

"Then the Lord answered Job out of the whirlwind. * * * Where wast thou when I laid the foundations of the earth? * * * Whereupon are the foundations thereof fastened? or who laid the cornerstone thereof, when the morning stars sang together, and all the sons of God shouted for joy? * * * Hast thou commanded the morning since the days, and caused the dayspring to know his place? Knowest thou the ordinances of heaven? Canst thou set the dominion thereof in the earth? * * * Wilt thou also disannul my judgment?"

Ah, poor Job! Thou wert able to maintain thy cause against Satan and against man, but what wilt thou answer to God? What, indeed, can Job say before this personal manifestation of God Himself but that which he did say:

"I have heard of thee by the hearing of

the ear; but now mine eye seeth thee. Wherefore I abhor myself."

THE UTTER COLLAPSE OF SELF

Yes, fellow-man, thyself. Now the secret is out.

It was not at all something Job had done, it was what Job was. Job himself was wrong. He had never judged self before God. He had not the sentence of death in himself. The interpretative chapter of Job is the twenty-ninth. The personal pronoun occurs forty-eight times in twenty-five verses. He was a good man, but he was too much aware of it, and he was in deep darkness as to the real state of his soul, of his inner life before God. And nothing, not the depth of his affliction, nor the reproaches of his friends, nor his own self-communings ever brought him to see himself. But when he passed from a knowledge *about* God to a personal acquaintance *with* God there was nothing to be said but the despairing:

"I have heard of thee by the hearing of the

ear, but now mine eye seeth thee. Wherefore I abhor myself."

The revelation of God, bringing a real sense of personal unworthiness and demerit, is what I think essentially we have in this experience of Job. It is not in exercises of self about self; not in any efforts of Job to discover the mystery of his inner life, that he comes to real self-consciousness; but it was the vision of God Himself which, flooding his inner being, brought the humbling, hateful vision of self.

A NEW AND HIGHER SERVICE

And then the most astonishing thing of all happened. God took up the vindication and restoration of the man who abhorred himself!

"The Lord said to Eliphaz the Temanite, My wrath is kindled against thee and against thy two friends: for ye have not spoken of me the thing that is right, as my servant Job hath."

And then, as you know, God made of Job a priest through whom alone the three reproachful moralizers could approach His offended holiness.

"My servant Job shall pray for you, and him will I accept."

You see, we have essentially four things here: First, the vision of God; secondly, the utter collapse of self; thirdly, a new and higher service; and lastly, a doubled fruitfulness.

"Also the Lord gave Job twice as much as he had before."

Now I believe we have here an order which is invariable, and I am very sure that we have here an experience which is not exceptional.

Oh, beloved, we too have heard of Him by the hearing of the ear, but we need to come to deeper things, closer things, with God. We need to come to that personal and underived acquaintanceship with Him, so that we may say with the men of Samaria, "Now we believe not because of thy saying; for we have heard him ourselves, and know that this is indeed the Christ," although the first effect of it will be this awful humbling, this utter collapse of self. But oh, how blessed a place is that valley of humbling. No one falls there who does not rise to newness of life and service. But re-

member, it costs the sentence of death in self;
the thorough reconstruction of the inner life.

NOT AN ISOLATED EXPERIENCE

It will help us in interpreting this experience
to see that it came, not to Job alone, but to
every man greatly used of God. The circumstances differ but the essence is the same—God
is realized, self-strength is turned into helpless-
ness, new power and blessing are given. Josh-
ua fell at the feet of the Man with the drawn
sword (Josh. 5:13-15); Isaiah must cry, "Woe
is me" (Isa. 6:5-8), only to be cleansed and
recommissioned; Jeremiah must learn that he
"cannot speak" before the Lord will touch his
mouth (Jer. 1:6-10); Ezekiel, prostrated by
the glory, must fall on his face in the collapse
of self before the Spirit can fill him, and Jehovah can say, "I send thee" (Ezek. 1:28;
2:1-10); Daniel must say, "I saw . . . and
my comeliness was turned in me into corrup-
tion" (Dan. 10:5-12). Even John the Beloved, before the vision of the glorified Christ,
must fall "at his feet as one dead" before the

"right hand" can be laid upon him, and he can hear the "fear not."

I wish now to gather up briefly what all this means. And first of all,

TWO THINGS WHICH IT IS NOT

It is neither the entire eradication of the flesh, the death, the extinction of self, nor is it sinless perfection. Self is abhored, distrusted, detested, set at naught. But so uniform are the characteristics of this experience, whatever the age or dispensation, that it is not difficult to state both the result accomplished and the steps by which it is wrought.

1. We have, then, in this supreme experience, the revelation of God Himself to the soul. It is not something about God; some new testimony concerning God, or some lesson of sorrow or trial. It is God's own act, His self-revelation of something which testimony had never communicated to heart or conscience, so that there is a new and intense apprehension of himself.

2. The instances quoted from the Scrip-

tures agree, too, in the effect of this unveiling
of God. Before that vision of God self is abhorred. So absolute is this effect that, as we
have seen, it is constantly spoken of as the utter deprivation of strength. The self-life is
not slain, but it is so seen in that glory as never
again to be trusted, or in any way counted on
in the things of God. As Paul said: "We had
the sentence of death in ourselves, that we
should not trust in ourselves, but in God, which
raiseth the dead," in the God of the resurrec-
tion, in the God of the new, undying life.

3.   In agreement, too, are the biblical instances that this destruction of self-confidence
is followed by the infilling with the strength
of Him who was dead and is alive again. Not
once is the man on his face before the awful,
beautiful vision left prostrate. "I received
strength," is the unvarying testimony.

4.   And then comes the new and higher service. This is the blessed consummation; this
and the new fruitfulness.

Could I covet anything better for you than
that you should see God face to face? Than

that there should come to you this highest word in the epic of the inner life? May He grant it, for His name's sake.

II

The Imparted Life

TEXT: "I am come that they might have life, and that they might have it more abundantly."—John 10:10.

THIS was the new note in the message of Jesus Christ. It fell, for the most part, upon uncomprehending ears. After nineteen centuries of alleged gospel preaching it is still for the most part uncomprehended.

That Christ was a teacher of ethics, as in the Sermon on the Mount, is understood. That He died for our sins is, as a fact, understood. That He changed the issue from righteousness by works to righteousness by faith, moving the centre from Mount Sinai in Arabia to Mount Calvary in Judea, is understood, though haltingly, but that He came to impart to believing human beings a new quality of life, even the very life which was and is in Himself—this is not understood.

Eternal life is, indeed, much spoken of, but

it is understood to mean mere duration of being—the persistency of life notwithstanding
the fact of physical death.

In the teaching of Jesus Christ, as in the
apostolic writings, the eternal life imparted by
Christ to all who believe in Him, is indeed a
term implying endlessness of life, but, since
endlessness is also a quality of mere human
life, eternal life is, far more emphatically, a
term of quality, of kind.

The ministry of John the Baptist also had
its startling message, "And now also the ax is
laid unto the root of the trees." There was
to be no more experimentation with the old
Adamic tree, no more seeking of fruit from a
stock that, after centuries of testing, could
produce but wild fruit. "Make the tree good"
is the new word, and this can only be done by
giving the tree a new life and nature. "That
which is born of the flesh is flesh," and can
never be made aught else. The old man under
the new gospel is to be crucified with Christ,
not improved by higher ideals. "They that
are in the flesh cannot please God." The
Adamic taint forbids it, and is ineradicable.

Two things are said by Christ in this tenth chapter of John: He gives his life *for* the sheep (vs. 11, 15, 17), and this is redemption; and He gives His life *to* the sheep (vs. 28) and this is regeneration.

Precisely this duality is found in the third chapter. The sheep are under a two-fold disability: they are "perishing" under the curse and sentence of the law, and must be redeemed by one able and willing to be "made a curse" in their stead; but also they are born of the flesh and therefore mere flesh-men, unable to "see" or "enter" the kingdom of God, and for this there is no remedy save in a re-birth.

But precisely these two needs are met by the gospel of the love of God; the Son of man must be lifted up on the cross to redeem the perishing, and the Holy Spirit imparts the divine nature and the new life to all who believe on the Son of man as crucified for their sins.

THE NEW LIFE IS CHRIST'S LIFE

Mere endlessness of being would not be "eternal" life. Eternal is "from everlasting to everlasting." Only He who "was in the begin-

ning with God * * * was God" could be-
stow, through the eternal Spirit, eternal life.

And this imparted life is His own life. "I
am the vine, ye are the branches." What a
symbol of unity of life is the vine with its
branches. The branch has no independent
source of life. The life of the vine and the life
of the branch are one. All possibility of renewal, of growth, of fruitfulness depends upon
the life energy of the vine. Well might the
vine say to the branch, "Because I live, ye shall
live also."

It would not be possible to state more
strongly than does our Lord this identity in
life of Himself and those who through faith
in Him crucified have been born again. "As *
* * I live by the Father: so he that eateth
me, even he shall live by me." "As thou,
Father, art in me, and I in thee, that they also
may be one in us." "I in them, and thou in
me."

The vital suggestions are, if possible, even
more intense in our Lord's simile of "the corn
of wheat." Just as a grain of wheat sown, dies
indeed, yet dies into countless grains of wheat,

giving its own life to each, so Christ speaks of His own death.

And this testimony to oneness of life with Christ pervades the apostolic explanation of the gospel. The church is declared to be His body. The human body, composed of many members, is the figure used to express the oneness with Him of the "many members" who constitute, like the members of the natural body, one organism, and this organism is called "Christ" (1 Cor. 12:12). It is declared of Christ, not only that He gave life to the believer, but that He "is our life." And John declares the record to be "that God hath given to us eternal life, and this life is in his Son."

THE INLIVING CHRIST TO BE OUTLIVED

God expects nothing from the flesh—the self-man. In the divine reckoning our old man was crucified with Christ. The old man is summed up in one terrific word of three letters—sin. Acts of sin proceed from a nature which is sin.

In one great and luminous passage the Holy Spirit through the Apostle Paul states, in the

terms of the apostle's actual experience, the
fact and method of the new life: "I am crucified with Christ." This is a fact of revelation
not a fact of consciousness. Paul does not
"feel" crucified, but in the divine reckoning he
is counted so, and this the apostle also reckons
to be true. God expects nothing from the old
Saul of Tarsus, and in the seventh of Romans
experience the apostle has learned the final
truth about Saul: "In me, that is in my flesh,
dwelleth no good thing."

Then comes a fact of consciousness, "Nevertheless I live," followed by another fact of
revelation, "Christ liveth in me." Saul lives as
yet, but death or the return of Christ will be
the end of the Saul life, and Christ also lives in
Paul.

Then comes the practical, present outcome
of it all, "The life which I now live in the
flesh" (body). How shall that life be lived?
The Holy Spirit gives an answer to which,
speaking broadly, the church has never risen.

THE METHOD OF THE CHRISTIAN LIFE

Two theories of Christian living here on

earth have measured, and do measure, the average faith.

First, life by precept, by rule. There is a large truth here. The Bible is a great instruction in righteousness; a great revelation of the mind of God about human life. No inner light can take the place of the divine revelation. It is perfect ethically and also complete.

But it has the fatal defect of furnishing no dynamic. "The law made nothing perfect." Precept gives a perfect rule of life, and by it life must always be tested, but precept carries no enablement. "The law * * * was weak through the flesh." A chart does not carry us across the ocean, but it shows us where we are on the trackless deep, and where to go. The life by precept was tried under law and left the whole world of humanity in speechless guilt before God.

Still more hopeless is the notion of life by the example of Christ. "What would Christ do?" is the formula. As to immoralities, selfishness, worldliness, the answer is easy. In all the real crises of life it utterly breaks down.

Our conclusions as to what Christ would do are vitiated by our limitations of habit of thought, of unspirituality, of ignorance of Christ. In His earth-life He constantly did the things that shocked every religionist in Palestine—Pharisee, Sadducee, Herodian. He did not do the things they thought He ought to do, but every day did something they thought inconsistent with His Messiahship.

What then is Christian living? It is Christ living out His life in the terms of our personality, and under the conditions which environ us. We do not ask, "What would Christ do?" we say to self, "Yet not I," and yield our powers to the sway of the inliving Christ. "Always bearing about in the body the putting to death of the Lord Jesus," (the practical expression of our co-crucifixion with Him being "having no confidence in the flesh"), "that the life also of Jesus might be made manifest in our body."

And we are not to be discouraged by failures. Not all at once does Christ gain complete control over powers and faculties accustomed to the rule of self; but, "walking in the Spirit," there assuredly comes an increasing sense of peace, rest, joy.

III

The Tragedy of the Inner Life

Text: "For to will is present with me, but how to perform that which is good, I find not."—Rom. 7:18.

THAT is the tragedy of the inner life; the breakdown of the human will before the Christian ethic; the torment of an unattained ideal.

The defeat of a languid desire is nothing; but to throw the whole power of the will on the side of something which God commands, and then to find the will break down, that, for an earnest soul, is tragic beyond words.

It is a very common mistake to suppose that we could be holy if we only wanted to. We think our difficulty lies in bringing the will to act on the side of what God requires, and that if we really put forth sufficient will power we should enter upon a spiritual life. But here is a man who makes the amazing discovery that the spiritual life is something

33

above the reach of his will at its highest
stretch. He can not grasp spirituality and
bring it down into his life by willing to do it.
And this was the experience, let us remember,
of one of the strongest wills that ever was
lodged in a human character. The Apostle
Paul was not a weakling; he was endowed
with immense will power.   When he was a
mere

RELIGIONIST AND NOT A CHRISTIAN

he was not a lax nor a languid one. He saw
that the great enemy of the traditionalism in
which he had been reared was this new thing,
Christianity; and his imperious will forced him
into the very front of the fight against Christianity; made of him "the tiger of the Sanhe-
drim." Nothing deterred him—no weeping of
women, no plaint of age, or youth; he put
Christian men and women in prison, and when
the question was one of stoning them to death
he gave his vote against them. No, Paul was
never a half-and-half man. There was in him
not merely a fullness of intellectual vigor and
life that compelled him to take sides, but there

was in him a force of will that enabled him to accomplish his desires.

But here was a seemingly simple thing that he was not able to do; but now he has before him an ideal which is unattainable by the power of his resolution. "To will is present with me," he says, "but how to perform that which is good, I find not." He can not will himself into spirituality.

WHAT IS "GOOD"?

That is the case before us. But we shall never understand what Paul means unless we stop for a moment to consider his little word "good." What is this good that Paul can not do by willing to do it? We may exclude some things at once. He is not speaking here of morality, of honesty, of kindliness, of chastity, of faithfulness in the relations in which man stands to man, as husband, as parent, as friend. These things lie completely within the power of the will. Every one of us has known men wholly apart from Christian power and Christian influence who were all of these things. Every community has upright, truthful, honest, kindly, courageous, helpful, clean, high-living men who are not Christians. The Apostle Paul is not speaking of those good qualities at all; all those things he had done all his life; his will had proved effective in that sphere.

And neither is he thinking, by this word *good,* of common religiousness, church-membership, church-going, saying prayers, reading the Bible, giving money; all these things he had done all his life by will power. He was the foremost religionist of his time, by a conscientious use of his will.

Well, then, what does he mean by speaking of the good which he wills but can not attain? He means such things as this: "For to me to live is Christ, and to die is gain." And this: "I am crucified with Christ; nevertheless I live; yet not I but Christ, liveth in me; and the life which I now live in the flesh, I live by the faith of the Son of God, who loved me and gave himself for me." That is what he is thinking about—the

REPRODUCTION OF CHRIST BEFORE MEN

—of being Christlike. That is what he calls "good." Did Paul mean, then, that he was defeated in a will to be Christlike—not as good *as* Christ, but good *like* Christ in measure? Yes.

He had before his mind, to illustrate it further, perhaps, the beatific character. He had read the Sermon on the Mount, and we may be very sure that he put it into its right place, dispensationally, but he was not willing for one moment to say that because he was in grace and in the church, and not in the kingdom and not under law, that therefore he was justified in living on a lower level than the kingdom life—rather he would say, "a higher demand is laid upon me."

And while there was not in his mind all this negative and inferior morality, there was in his mind the spiritual morality which forms the Christian standard. "Blessed are the poor in spirit," he would say, and then I can imagine that he would beat upon his breast and say, "Oh, proud Paul! Oh, Paul, when will you ever be poor in spirit?" And then, perhaps, in the earlier stages of his experience he would say, "I *will* be poor in spirit."

"Blessed are the meek." "Oh," he would say afterward, "I am the chief of sinners. When I read that word *meek,* I dare not lift my eyes to him—I can not." Did you, my hearer, ever try to be meek? If you did, did you succeed? It is open to any one to act meekly, to go around with a kind of

URIAH HEEP 'UMBLENESS

but that only makes a hateful Pharisee of you; that is not being meek. And if there is anything that Jesus Christ hates, it is Phariseeism; that is the one thing He can not do anything with. The only word he had for the Pharisee of his day was, "Woe unto you." He had no messages for them; there was nothing in his gospel for a Pharisee. No, Paul is not going back to Phariseeism. And, deeper than that there was in Paul's heart, when he talked about being "good," the imperious demand which his new nature and the urge of the new life made upon him that he should have victory over self in all the forms in which self manifests itself.

Now in the face of a standard as exalted as the Christlike life there is

A GRAVE DANGER

That danger must have been present to Paul, and I have no doubt he had to resist it and to cry mightily to God about it; the danger, I mean, of saying or thinking that the Christ standard is too high; that it was put there, not to attain to, but as an ideal toward which we are to aspire. We are to consent to it that it is good, but for flesh to expect to attain to it is another thing. Well, here was a man who was minded to live that kind of a life, somehow, and never let himself go till he did.

There is a saying, you know, that if you aim your arrow at the moon you won't hit the moon, but you will shoot higher than if you aimed your arrow at a barn. Well, Paul never let himself down by any poor sophistry like that. You and I do, my friends.

Now I want to pass on to

A VERY PRACTICAL QUESTION

What does Paul mean by saying, "To will is present with me, but how to perform that which is good, I find not"? I have heard all my Christian life the statement that Christians are not to live in the seventh of Romans. Well, I would to God that nine out of ten of them got into the seventh of Romans. The man in the seventh of Romans is not a listless dweller in spiritual things; he is a man whose heart is breaking and whose being is in agony because his life is not like Christ's! The man in the seventh of Romans is a man who was all red with the blood of the Son of God. He knew that he was wrestling with something that was awful and real, and he was bound to have the solution for this problem if God has one for him. I ask, what does this man need who wills and resolves to do good, and then finds himself defeated? Does he need more ethics? A higher standard? Why, the poor man knows more good now than he is doing; and just there is the weakness of mere ethical preaching. It continually says to the poor

sinner, "Be good," but never tells him how to
be good. And the pulpit today is largely en-
gaged with telling people to "be good" and not
telling them how.

We come to him with the Ten Commandments and say, "Why, Paul, I do not know
what is the matter with you; you seem beside
yourself with all this talk about not being able
to be good. Here are the Commandments."
And he says, "But I know them; I have known
them from my youth up, and I delight in them
after the inner man, but I can not keep even
them." No, law can not help him. Law says,
"Thou shalt," and "Thou shalt not," but it
adds nothing to the force and power of man;
nothing whatever. Well, what does he need?

NOT ETHICS, BUT DYNAMICS

The man needs superhuman power to enable
him to realize in his life a superhuman spirituality.

Now, when any one says, as an objection to
Christianity, that the ethical demand of Christianity is too high or human nature, he has
just begun to find out the truth; a truth that

about eight out of every ten Christians never do find out. It is too high for human nature. It is meant to be too high for human nature. It is put where no hand of man can ever touch it; where no unassisted human capacity can ever reach it. And if that were all, the gospel would be to the saint, whatever• it may be to the sinner, a message of despair. But that is not all.

Along with this superhuman demand, superhuman power is offered. And Paul laid hold upon it. He did not stay in the seventh of Romans, for when the will is aroused to its utmost power and yet can not do a thing, then the man has reached the end of himself.

AT PEACE AND VICTORIOUS

When we pass from the seventh to the eighth of Romans we find the wretched man of the seventh of Romans at peace and victorious; what is now his testimony? "The law of the spirit of life in Christ Jesus hath made me free from the law of sin and death." Not a new resolution, nor a new habit, nor a deeper hold on himself, nor more prayer. Do you think that a man in the agony of the seventh of Romans does not pray? Why, the Apostle Paul, when he was there, prayed, you may be sure, day and night on his face before God. Not more prayer, nor more anything that you and I can do, nor that Paul could do, but something that God can do.

THERE IS THE REMEDY

That is what Paul means: not more from within, but something from without put within. And almost while he is saying, "Oh, wretched man that I am," out of the very agony of spiritual defeat, he lifts up his face in triumphant testimony for he has found the secret, and he says, "The law of the spirit of life in Christ Jesus hath made me free from the law of sin and death" (Rom. 8:2).

So this man can write afterward, "For me to live is Christ"; write it to Philippians who knew him more intimately than you know me. "The life which now I live in the flesh, I live by the faith of the Son of God he could say to those Galatians who had seen him under trial and testing, "Not by my efforts, nor by my resolutions, nor by my vows, but by the power, the authority, the law, of the spirit of life in Christ Jesus."

Defeated along the line of the will, he is victorious by the power of the Spirit within him; the superhuman standard achieved by superhuman power. Paul laid hold upon that power, and so we have the triumphant eighth chapter of Romans, which may be the experience of every child of God—a life of continual victory, peace and power.

IV

The Delivered Life

TEXT: "If the Son therefore shall make you free, ye shall be free indeed."—John 8:36.

THE most widespread and universal of the delusions current among men is the notion that they are free. No imputation is more quickly, more vehemently resented than the imputation of slavery, of bondage. There are no free men. Millions, thank God, are in the process of emancipation, but none are yet completely emancipated. Paul told the Roman chief captain that he was born free. In the limited sense in which he used the word it was true; Paul was born a Roman citizen. But in every other important sense the words were not true, as Paul would have been the first to admit. Like all of us, Paul inherited chains. For centuries that mysterious force, heredity, had been silently, invisibly, preparing bonds for him—bonds for spirit, soul, body. Every soul born into the

45

world is born into an invisible net which the
centuries have been weaving for him. Its
meshes are race predisposition, race habit, family habit, sin, formal religion, and, "they say."

Think of the men to whom Christ was talk-
ing when He uttered the words of our text.
"We be Abraham's seed, and were never in
bondage to any man." They spoke honestly
enough, as we do when we boast of our freedom, but at that moment they were in political,
intellectual and religious bondage.

Politically, they were under bondage to an
assortment of despots from Caesar down to
Herod and Pilate. Morally, they were the
slaves of race pride, of prejudice, of ignorance,
of habit, of sin, of self-will. Religiously, they
were the slaves of traditionalism, of bigotry, of
formalism.

WE ARE SLAVES OF PARTY

Is our case better? Very slightly. Theoret-
ically, we are free politically. Actually, we are
the slaves of party, of the caucus, of the bosses.
The very minute I give over into the hands of
a convention the right to formulate my polit-

ical creed I am no longer absolutely free. When I take my opinions, my convictions, concerning morals or religion second-hand from other men, whether they are men of today or men of the Reformation period, or of the early church council, I am no longer free.

When I allow a habit to dominate my life, I am no longer free. When I allow pride or vanity, or ambition, or pleasure to control my life, I am the basest of slaves. The very fact that I do not, can not, of myself, cease from sin proclaims me a slave. Jesus Christ came into a world of slaves.

CHRIST THE EMANCIPATOR

It is interesting to note that His first formal announcement of His mission on earth touched life at that very point. In the synagogue at Nazareth there was handed to Him the book of the Prophet Isaiah, and He found the place where it was written: "The spirit of the Lord is upon me, because he hath anointed me to preach * * * deliverance to the captives."

He begins with our slavery to sin. And here

He encounters an initial difficulty. The man whom He would set free is not only a slave, but a condemned slave. He is a slave, exposed for sale, but with a halter round his neck. Who will redeem him? Nay, rather, who can redeem him? Not his brother man, for he too is a slave with a halter round his own neck. "What is the price of this slave? of that one?" One price for all. Whoever will redeem these slaves must die in their stead. And, obviously, only one who has never sinned, and who is himself perfectly free, can be accepted. Only one being has ever appeared who met these necessary conditions—Jesus Christ. And, to pay that price is the very business that brought Jesus Christ to this earth. At the cost of His own life, of His own unimaginable suffering, He pays the last demand of a holy law and redeems from death the slaves of sin.

Are they free from the curse of the law? Yes. From the habit of sin? No. Then begin those great redemptive processes which work in the sphere of the inner life, the object of which is the transformation of character and complete deliverance from the *dominion* of sin.

THE PROCESS OF DELIVERANCE

It begins with the complete removal of fear. The believer is told that he is not under law, that is, a system of probation to see if he can work out a righteousness for himself, but under grace, that is, a system of divine inworking, which produces the very righteousness which the law required, but which man never achieved. The believer is assured that Christ has given to him eternal life, and that he shall never perish; that nothing is able to pluck him out of the omnipotent hand which holds him; that He who began a **good work in him** will perfect it till the day of Christ. As for his sins; they are blotted out, cast behind God's back, buried in the depths of the sea, forgiven and forgotten. And this is a necessary first work, for no man is really free who is under the bondage of fear.

Then grace imparts to the believer the indwelling Holy Spirit. The nature that was open to every assault from without, and a slave to every vile impulse from within is now garrisoned by omnipotence. In the power of that

indwelling One, the believer is made free from
the monstrous necessity of sinning under which
every unredeemed life groans. No Christian
needs to sin. If he yields to solicitations from
without, or the more subtle suggestions from
within, it is because he deliberately or care-
lessly wills it so. The Spirit is there to break
the power of sin.

GRACE AND THE INSPIRATION OF NEW RELATION-
SHIP

Then grace puts the renewed life under the
stimulus and inspiration of great relationships.
The believer is not merely a pardoned criminal,
he is a child and son of God; and that by a new
birth which is as actual in the sphere of the
spiritual as his natural birth was in the sphere
of the physical. He is a son of God, not by
some far-off fact of creation, but by the imme-
diate and personal fact of a divine begetting.
He no longer traces his descent from God
through Adam, but is, as Adam was, a son of
God with no intervening ancestor.

This, the believer is told, brings him into the
wonderful privileges of access to the Father,

and of fellowship with Him. Christ is not ashamed to call him "brother"; he is raised to joint heirship with Christ in all things, and is to share the power and glory of Christ in the coming kingdom.

Grace confers upon the believer the great offices of priest and king. As priest he is set free from the ancient formalism in the worship of God "entering into the holiest by the blood of Jesus," and offering, without regard to time or place, "spiritual sacrifices, acceptable unto God through Jesus Christ." His worship, freed from ceremonialism, is a son's adoration of a Father who is infinite in holiness and benevolence and power, but who is none the less a Father because He is God. And this office of priest carries of necessity the privilege of intercession. The believer-priest prays for those outside the family of God who do not pray for themselves. He, like Christ, is the daysman and remembrancer before his Father of the unbelieving world.

Grace tells the believer that he is as vitally united to Christ as the members of his own body are united to him. "By one Spirit are we all baptized into one body." "He that is joined unto the Lord is one Spirit."

WHAT TRUE FREEDOM IS

But Christian freedom is not anarchy, which is the mere riot of self-will, but it is to be so joined to God the Father; so vitally one with Christ the Son; so yielded to the gentle sway of the Holy Spirit, that the human will is blended into the divine will, and so made one with the absolutely free and sovereign will of God Himself. God does as He wills, but God always wills to do that which is at once absolutely right and absolutely benevolent.

And in all this there is no subversion of the believer's individuality, but the lifting of that individuality to the divine level of a passionate love of all that is lovely. It is obedience, but obedience under the new covenant, where the law is written in the heart, like mother-love. A mother finds her highest joy in obedience to that imperative born into her deepest being with the birth of her child.

No truly honest man feels the constraint of the laws against theft. He is not honest because of something printed in a statute book, but because of something printed on his heart. He would still be honest if the statute were repealed. And therefore he is perfectly free. Without that interior work no external thing done to a man makes or can make him free. Executive clemency extended to a convicted criminal does not make him a free man. He is still the slave of his criminal desires. But if he falls in love with honesty and uprightness and integrity, then he is free. All this transformation grace works in the redeemed heart.

THE NEW IDEAL OF LIFE

Then grace works transformingly by the power of new and exalted ideals. The whole conception of life is changed. Under the old bondage life was conceived of as a possession which man might rightly use for himself; under the new ideal, life is precious because it may be used for the blessing of others. The new man in Christ has accepted as the new ideal of his new life Christ's law of sacrifice. He heartily adopts Christ's formula: "The Son of man came not to be ministered unto, but to minister, and to give his life a ransom for many"; "He that will save his life shall lose it, but he that will lose his life for my sake, shall find it"; "Except a corn of wheat fall into the ground and die, it abideth alone, but if it die, it bringeth forth much fruit."

Such an ideal, heartily accepted, under the conviction that so only may life be nobly lived, works of itself toward disenthralment from the old slavery of self.

Pursued, though with many a failure, and with steps which often halt, such an ideal is a transformation. The man who accepts it has issued to the universe his declaration of independence. He is free from the old appeals and solicitations which had power over him because they seemed to promise something toward the old monstrous ministry to the god self. No longer desiring self-exaltation or self-pleasing, the bribe has ceased to appeal. Its presentment only causes pain to the heart that has fallen in love with humility.

THE VISION OF ETERNITY

Then grace allures and charms with the

vision of eternal things. Paul divides all things
into two categories, things seen and things unseen, and he declares that the seen things have
the fatal defect of being temporary, while the
unseen things have the infinite value of eternal endurance. Believing this, the new man in
Christ sits lightly to things seen. They become
the mere incidents of life, not its substance. Of
this world's goods he may have much, and he
is glad because they can be used to enrich other
lives; or he may gather little, and he is glad
because he has not the responsibility of the
right use of great possessions. His true inheri-
tance is in heaven. And in and through all
this the Son has made him free.

Walking in the Spirit, the Lord's free-man
has but to heed the exhortation, "Stand fast,
therefore, in the liberty wherewith Christ hath
made us free, and be not entangled again with
the yoke of bondage."

V

The Larger Christian Life

Text: "He brought me forth also into a large place."—Psa. 18:19.

YOU observe that we have here a testimony, not a promise. God actually had done this thing for David. He was a shepherd lad; obscure, conscious but dimly if at all of his own capacities; shut up to the small things and small thoughts of a young rustic. Then God began to work in his life, stimulating him with great promises, leading him into great ventures, beating him with the hammer of adversity till the crude ore of him was turned into tempered steel; but all the while breaking shackles, tearing away enmeshing nets, lifting the wings of his soul, filling him with divine inbreathings, expanding, enlarging, disenthralling him; until at last David came to the consciousness that he was a free man and in a large place. He could stand with lifted head, strong young arms outflung, upraised chest breathing deep the free, ample air, a man at home in the universe. I repeat it, David is testifying here, not theorizing. He had found it so. Upon which I remark:

THE REAL CHRISTIAN LIFE IS LARGE

It is the men who are living without God who are living in a small and narrow place. There is no more shameless lie afloat among men than that the Christian life is a narrow life, and that the life that does not subject itself to the will of God is a high, free thing.

We are all, I believe, passionate lovers of liberty. We seek room; we want a place in which we may expand and broaden out. A great many young people of today have a fancy that to come into the will of God is to come into narrowness. It is Satan's lie. But let us not blame the devil overmuch. He never could have got his lie believed if so many of God's people had not made "religion" a poor negative thing: a system of "don't" and of outward observance.

It was to intensely "religious" people—in

this sense—that Christ spoke His great word, "If the Son, therefore, shall make you free, ye shall be free indeed." He came to preach deliverance to the captive of formalism no less than to the captive of sin. The gospel is a call out of littleness, out of pettiness, out of insignificent things, to the breadth and sweep of great thoughts and forces, and to the wide horizon of limitless possibilities.

Now it is true of every child of God that he is brought into a large place. Unfortunately, many persist in living narrow lives in the large place. To be free and not to know it, this seems to me tragical and pathetic beyond words. One thinks of old prisoners set free, and weeping for the old dungeon again.

CIRCUMSTANCES CANNOT NARROW IT

Just here permit me to anticipate a very natural objection. You say, "I live in obscurity; God has set me in narrow circumstances, in a routine of petty duties. I live in a farm house; I live in a village; I toil in a factory; I monotonously feed pieces of leather or wood into a machine and never see them again; I plow, I delve, I sell cloth by the yard, I wash pans and dishes. I know of no large and beautiful way to wash pans. I keep a little district school; I must have my mind on my work; my back grows bent and my muscles stiff and sore. I am no exultant young David, anointed of the Lord, free to go and come, to sing deathless songs, to rule over men."

PATIENCE, DEAR HEART, HEAR THIS

Jesus Christ lived thirty years in Nazareth, but He never permitted Nazareth to give the measure of His life. You may think of Him as a boy helping His mother, holding baby, fetching water from the fountain and chips from the shop. He made yokes, I suppose, not wholesale with a big iron machine, but one by one, patiently fitting them to peasant shoulders, broad and narrow, stooped and straight. Thirty years He lived there, and there was matured the finest human character the world ever saw. The baptism with the Spirit added power; suffering perfected sympathy, but it was the largest, freest man that ever lived who laid down His carpenter's tools one day and walked down to Jordan to be baptized of John.

Do you not see the secret? He never permitted Nazareth to put its littleness upon Him. The one man upon whom there are no limitations whatever of race, of circumstance or of character was a villager who toiled for bread!

It is not given to many of us to live in great scenes and to be a part of great transactions. Our life is a round of small cares and duties. But Jesus Christ lived in narrower circumstances than ours. The newspapers, the telegraph, the railway and steamship bring largesses to the remotest of us. Homer chanted his deathless songs from door to door, in poverty, unappreciated, for a crust of bread. Milton, shut up to physical blindness, ranged in spirit from the Paradise that was to the Paradise that shall be. Dante, in exile, in a petty, mediæval town, learning "the steepness of another's stairs and the saltness of another's bread," fathomed the upper and the nether depths.

Do you say, "But we are not Homer, Milton, and Dante?" Thank God! I would rather have my two eyes than Milton's fame; my own good native land than Dante's exile; my humble home than Homer's wanderings. But surely our souls have some power of flight; their wings may beat the upper air for some distance, somewhere, if they may not take Dante's tremendous spirals.

WHAT WE ARE, NOT WHAT WE DO, DETERMINES
THE LARGENESS OF LIFE

Lacordaire says: "A king may pass through our streets clothed in purple and fine linen, and he may be a mean and base man, because his thoughts are mean and base; and there may pass by a poor man in vile raiment and he may be a great man, because his converse with himself is high and great." That is true. Things do not make life large. Men do large things sometimes in small places, and others do small things in large places. If we are of kin to the great souls we shall some time be known as of that strain.

A homely American poet has put this into his poem: "The Unexpressed." Three men, writer, musician, builder, plod through life, toiling day by day for daily bread; and the writer never pens the epic which he dumbly feels; the musician never composes the oratorio which resounds in his soul; the builder builds wooden houses instead of the cathedral of which he feels himself capable and then they die, and the three men who greet them are Homer, Mozart, and Michel Angelo!

> "This dead musician's soul went forth
>   Into the darkness drear—
> A glad voice smote the clouds apart—
> The brother-greeting of Mozart,
>   Who hailed him as his peer.
> 'Souls know,' he said, 'that music best
> That haunts the dumb soul unexpressed.' "

Yes; many a life of obscurity, poverty, neglect, self-denial and pain is essentially great because it is lived in fellowship with great things—the things of God. Such a soul can wait. It is elect, and shall yet come to its own.

"Serene, I fold my hands and wait,
    Nor care for wind, or tide, or sea;
I rave no more 'gainst time or fate,
    For, lo, my own shall come to me.

"I stay my haste, I make delays;
    For what avails this eager pace?
I stand amid the eternal ways,
    And what is mine shall know my face.

"Asleep, awake, by night and day,
    The friends I seek are seeking me.
No wind shall drive my bark astray,
    Nor change the tide of destiny.

"What matter if I stand alone?
    I wait with joy the coming years;
My heart shall reap where it has sown,
    And garner up its fruit of tears.

"The waters know their own and draw
    The brook that springs in yonder height;
So flows the good with equal law
    Unto the soul of pure delight.

"The stars come nightly to the sky,
    The tidal waves unto the sea;
Nor time, nor tide, nor deep, nor high,
    Shall keep my own away from me!"

THE SECRET OF THE LARGER LIFE

If now you ask me how all this larger Christian life may be lived, I shall venture three suggestions:

1. Put your life under the great law of exclusion by preoccupation. Keep littleness out by being with greatness. There was no place in Christ for mean things. It was not that Christ refused small cares, drudgeries, duties. It was that He accepted them and was filled with the joy of doing them.

2. Live your Christian life in the sense of its great verities. You are children and heirs of God by faith in Jesus Christ. Say every day, "I am a child of God." I defy circumstances to narrow and dwarf the life that is lifted by the consciousness of divine sonship and divine fellowship.

"The larger Christian life is independent of circumstances."

There drifted into my house once a human wreck. He had been the editor of a great daily newspaper, and was a man of rare gifts. It was the old story; little by little the drink habit had fastened upon him and had dragged him down to a living hell. I could not tell him to "assert his manhood;" he had none. I had a better gospel than that. I told him that he could be born again; that he could become a partaker of the divine nature, and a son and heir of God. He fell upon his knees. "My God!" he cried. "Can a dog like me become God's son?" And he poured out his heart, giving himself away to Christ. I shall never forget his transfigured face, nor the singular solemnity and loftiness of his bearing as he took my hand and said: "I am a child of God."

Get out under the stars on a clear night, and look over your estate. The stars are yours and Christ's. Know that as a child of God you are greater than any possible estate, and you will not wash pans, plow and reap any less thoroughly, but you will do these things royally, like a king or queen. Remember, you are of the family of God.

A poor saint went into a very aristocratic church in a strange place. "I believe," said the usher rather dubiously, "that I do not know you." "Do you know the Lord Jesus Christ?"

asked the poor saint. "Oh, yes." "Well," said the poor man, "I am a poor brother of His."

3.   Be a vital part of Christ's work.

"The field is the world." Your field is the world. Keep your sympathies world wide. If your heart is in China or Africa or Central America, and with the work there, it is just the same as if you were there, wherever your body may happen to be.

At the Student Volunteer Convention in Cleveland they had Carey's cobbler's hammer. It was better worth seeing than the crown jewels in the Tower. No scepter in Christendom is so venerable as that hammer. It is as if it came out of the shop in Nazareth, almost. Carey beat hobnails into peasants' shoes with that hammer; beat sturdily and well. But, as one thinks of him, the narrow walls of his cobbler's stall fall away, and his humble bench changes to the likeness of a throne, and one sees a pierced hand hold over his head the diadem of righteousness. For that cobbler, bowed over his daily task, was sweeping the darkened continents into his yearning, and holding a world up in prayer to God.

VI

The Spirit-Controlled Life

TEXT: "Whosoever drinketh of the water that I shall give him shall never thirst; but the water that I shall give him shall be in him a well of water springing up into everlasting life."—John 4:14.

L ET us think of the Holy Spirit and the inner life of the believer. There is an inner life; an inner life so deep, so truly inner, that no one knows it but God and ourselves. It is a life of which, in its deeper depths, we never speak to our dearest friends. There are defeats there, there are victories there—heart-surgings, heartaches that we cannot put into words—we can only go with them before God, and the Spirit, who helpeth our infirmities, can make intercession for us with groanings which cannot be uttered.

Now, we are to think of the Holy Spirit as indwelling the believer:

THE UPSPRINGING FOUNTAIN WITHIN

What a wonderful symbol it is! How apart

from all other instructions, it speaks of the constant renewal of the spiritual life. You know the contrast was with Jacob's well, which was very deep, and out of which water must be laboriously drawn. When our Lord spoke to the woman about this living water, this water which was not down in the bottom of the well, but was upspringing, she asked a question: "Whence hast thou this water? Thou hast nothing to draw with and the well is deep."

What a contrast, what a picture of the average Christian life! Somehow, if we are Christians at all, we get on; we manage to get through the day after a fashion, but it is just like that poor woman, laboriously drawing water out of Jacob's well. We draw it up just a little at a time, and some of us with a sense that we have nothing to draw with, and there is a constant effort to be spiritual; and over against that our Lord puts the picture of a fountain that springs up of its own lovely energy, and throws its crystal flood into the clear air and dances and sparkles there in the sunlight, and then flows away to be kissed by the sun back again into the azure blue.

Now the Christian life, the true spiritual life in Christ's conception of it, is a life which has *within* it the source and renewal of its freshness and vigor and power. An upspringing fountain constantly fed from a higher source, coming down that it may ascend again. Here is a little springlet in the valley half afraid that it may dry up; and the spring up on the mountain says: "No, you shall not dry up, for I am renewing your abundance all the time." What a contrast with the average life! Here is the plentitude of divine power, the omnipotent Spirit of God, who has not only taken up his abode in us, but wishes to be in the believer a living vital force, constantly renewed, himself the unwasting Source.

Now, is our Christian life like that, or do we have to painfully draw it with a creaking windlass out of Jacob's well till our backs ache? Which is it? There is the contrast.

SOURCE HIGHER THAN ITSELF

And, too, the inlet must be kept open and the outlet must be kept open.

There are two sins which Christians commit

against the Spirit. We are said to grieve the Spirit, and we are told some of the things which grieve Him. "Grieve not the Holy Spirit of God, whereby ye are sealed unto the day of redemption. Let all bitterness and wrath and anger and clamor and evil speaking be put from you with all malice." Now are you allowing a little bitter feeling toward somebody in your heart? Bitterness! Wrath! Anger! Perhaps we do not care much about that. We say, "The Lord knows I was born with a hot temper; I am made up that way, but it is just a flash and all over in a minute." All over with you, perhaps, but is it all over with the heart you have wounded? Anger! Malice! Envy! Ah, my friends, all these things which we allow in ourselves, defended, petted, kept there, are but stones that choke the inlet and prevent the upspringing of the fountain.

And then we are told not to quench the Spirit; not to say "No" to the Spirit, but to let the Spirit have His way. To say "No" when the Spirit says, "Pray, serve, give," is to choke the outlet, and the fountain does not flow. Now

JUST A FEW PROPOSITIONS

Do not imagine that your Jacob's well experience proves that you have not the fountain within you. In other words, don't imagine, if you are a believer on the Lord Jesus Christ, that you have not the Spirit within. Every believer of the Lord Jesus Christ is indwelt by the Holy Spirit. You have not to intercede for Him, you have not to seek Him, you have but to take account of the fact that you have Him already. "What?" says Paul in the sixth chapter of 1 Corinthians, "Know ye not that your body is the temple of the Holy Ghost, which is in you, which ye have of God, and ye are not your own?" And remember, the apostle is addressing there a people whom he has just described as "carnal'—running after human leaders—babes in Christ, to these he says, "What? Know ye not that your body is the temple of the Holy Ghost which is in you, which ye have of God, and ye are not your own?"

Now, when that fact is received by faith, without waiting for feeling, you have taken a long step toward better things. If you really believe that the Holy Spirit of God dwells in your mortal body, a transformation of life has begun.

WHAT THE UPSPRINGING FOUNTAIN DOES

First, the Spirit indwells the believer that he may give victory over the old self-life. A mightier power has come in and while the old, evil life of the flesh is there, omnipotence is holding it in the place of death and we may be free from the dominion of it. Not by good resolutions, not by struggling to keep a law, but by divine power within, to which we have yielded our whole being. Ah, it is a deep truth that old John Newton uttered when he said, "I hear a great deal of talk about the pope, but the pope who troubles me most is Pope John Newton." Now, the Spirit of God is there to govern, to control, to keep that self life in the place of death and to give us victory as we walk in the Spirit.

And secondly, He is there to make real the things of Christ. "He shall receive of mine," as the promise was, "and show it unto you."

Now that does not mean "exhibit," but "make actual" to us the things of Christ.

And thirdly, He is here to make real to you the Fatherhood of God. You realize that God is your Father by the Holy Spirit. And when you pray to God you are not merely praying to a Creator, to one who laid the foundations of the earth and who keeps the planets in their courses, but you are praying to your Father in heaven; and just as you go to an earthly father with your needs, wanting help and counsel, just so you may go to your heavenly Father. So, because the Spirit of sonship dwells in you, you realize the Fatherhood of God.

Furthermore, the Spirit will take up every one of the blessings which we have in Christ and give us possession of them.

And when He is ungrieved and unquenched, He is doing that. That is the life in the Spirit.

And then he takes up the problems, the difficulties that we have to do within our lives and settles them for us according to the will of God; so that the outer life is the unforced expression of an inner life which is pure and clean and high, and full of love and tenderness, looking about with the eyes of love on all humanity, watching for opportunities to put out the helping hand and to lift up the downtrodden and oppressed.

The whole problem lies, not in self-effort, not in painfully drawing water out of Jacob's well—that is going back to the law; to what the apostle calls the "beggarly elements of the world"; to elementary things—and not going on to the fulness of what God has for us. Which is it to be hereafter? The upspringing fountain, or Jacob's well?

VII

The Joyous Life

TEXT: "That they might have my joy fulfilled in themselves."—John 17:13.

WE have here two simple ideas—Jesus Christ filled with joy; ourselves privileged to partake of that joy until we also are filled.

PLEASURE, HAPPINESS, JOYOUSNESS

It is not uncharitable to say that many people in this world are content if they may be merry; they seek nothing higher from life than pleasure. If they may put far from them the burden and sorrow and care of this world, and forget its grief in a passing jest, they are content. There is a place in life for pleasure, but pleasure is never the object of lives which are noble.

Better than this and the pursuit, I would fain believe, of a far great number, is happiness. Happiness is an infinitely higher thing than pleasure, and the desire of God that His children should be happy is abundantly revealed in the Bible. The Beatitudes are instructions in the art of happiness.

But our text speaks of something which is better even than happiness, and that is joyousness. Joyousness, in the scriptural sense of the word, might be defined as happiness overflowing. Happiness too full to be used up in mere personal satisfaction; happiness all alive and aglow. If happiness might be compared to a tranquil lake, embosomed in protecting hills, joyousness would be like the outflowing of a brimming river.

It may, then, help us just at the beginning, to fix in our minds these three things which stand over against sorrow or pain; pleasure, which exists for and ends upon self; happiness, a deeper, nobler thing, and joyousness, which is the overflow of happiness.

THE JOY OF JESUS CHRIST

First of all, Jesus speaks of His own joy. Now, we do not habitually think of Jesus Christ as joyful. Long before His manifestation, the Prophet Isaiah had said of Him that He would be a "man of sorrows and acquainted with grief." And so it was. But observe: A man of sorrows, not a man of melancholy. We can not think of Jesus Christ as moping through life; we can not think of Him as turning fretfully toward His burden, as thinking of His wrongs—His throne denied Him, His people rejecting Him, His poverty and humiliation in a world which He had made. Just once, in Gethsemane, He speaks of His sorrows: "My soul is exceedingly sorrowful, even unto death." But habitually He speaks of His joyfulness. That, then, is the paradox of His life. "A man of sorrows and acquainted with grief"; but bearing these sorrows, as it were, upon the deep floodtide of a mighty joy. And the joy was more than the sorrow.

Let us try to understand this paradox—an exultant and joyful man of sorrows.

Have you ever observed that the nearer Jesus came to the cross, the more He spoke of His joy? You do not find that He testified of His joyfulness much in the earlier part of His ministry, and I believe not once in that which is called "the year of public favor," when the multitudes thronged Him, and it seemed as if the nation would really receive Him as the long-expected Messiah. But as He went on, drawing ever nearer to Calvary, and as the burden of the shame and sorrow and sin of the world began to gather in awful darkness over Him, He speaks ever more and more of His joyfulness, and in His closing admonitions and instruction there is a constant reference to the deep joy which filled His being. Just when the tide of sorrow is rising highest, the joyfulness seems to rise above it and triumph over it.

THE PARADOX SOLVED

If we ponder that, and connect it with the prophet's explanation of the sorrows of Jesus Christ, "Surely he hath borne our griefs, and carried our sorrows," I think we shall be on the very verge of solving the paradox. In other words (and is it not very simple?), Jesus found His supreme joy in bearing the sorrows of others. He was not joyful in spite of having to bear the sorrow and burden of the

world; He was joyful because He *could* bear
it. It was the fountain head, the very source,
of His joy.

I think we can conceive of that, if we are
willing to separate ourselves for a moment
from that shrinking which we all feel at the
thought of pain and sorrow, and get upon the
nobler side of our own souls. We can understand that such a being as Jesus would rejoice, with joy unspeakable, that He *could* do
that thing. We can understand how, when
looking down upon this world, with its sin
and misery and want and woe, and mountain-
ous iniquity, there would be ever in His heart
the exultant joy at knowing that it was He
who, in due time, should come down here and
get underneath all that unspeakable guilt and
bear it away from man through the cross.

Just as Jean Valjean, in Victor Hugo's
great story, was happy under the cart; it hurt
him cruelly, but he lifted it away from the
old man who was being crushed by it. So
there was a joy in the very pain which it cost
to do it—the joy of vicarious suffering; the
joy of getting underneath all that was bearing

down the heart of humanity, and lifting it forever away—this was the joy of the Lord.

You know how easily, after all, poor as this world is in nobleness, this truth finds illustration. Surely, Winkelreid must have felt something of that joy when he gathered the spears of the enemy into his own bosom so that his comrades might break the hostile line and make way for liberty. There must have been in him an ineffable joy as he felt those spears crushing into his heart and his life going out. There was suffering, but it was a joyful thing so to die.

I think that pilot, who kept his burning boat against the shore until every passenger was safe, though his own hands burnt to a crisp as he held the wheel, must have had a joy greater than the pain. This is a very high kind of joy, but we may realize it after all, may we not?

I think that captain who stood upon the deck of the sinking ship and gave his place in the last boat to a poor stowaway, who had no kind of claim upon him, and saw him pass on into safety while he went down with the ship, drank deeply of this joy of vicarious suffering.

SOURCES OF THE SAVIOUR'S JOY

Then there was another source of the joy of the Lord. He rejoiced in the will of God. Will you consider that for a moment? What a joyful thing it is that we are not left alone in this world! What a joyful thing to know that one is not the sport of circumstance and of accident; not orphaned amid all these destructive forces that move in upon us, as children of God here in the world; to know, in short, that over it all there is the resistless will of God. Things are not "happening" to the children of God. We are moving upon an appointed course, and the joys and sorrows of our lives are all appointed and portioned out, molding and shaping us for better things. The joy of doing and enduring the will of God, and of suffering that others might not suffer—here are the abiding sources of our Lord's joy.

In the Hebrews we are told of another source of joy which sustained our Lord in the supreme agony of the cross—"the joy that was set before him." The joy of the final consummation; the joy of anticipation when He should see the eternal results of His suffering; all this was present with Him helpfully in the hour of agony. That is what we need to see. Beyond question we do not live enough in the inspiration of the compensations and balancings of heaven.

THE LORD'S JOY, OUR JOY

Turn now for a moment to the other thought —the human side of it.

"That my joy might be fulfilled in them."

But how shall we have the joy of the Lord? Evidently there is here a call to the unselfish heights? If we are to share the joy of the Lord we must be willing to share that out of which His joy sprang. We must rejoice if we can bear away some sorrow from another heart, some burden from another life, even if it means sorrow and burden to us.

We must learn to rejoice as we never yet have learned to rejoice, in the salvation of the lost. We read that there is "joy in the presence of the angels of God over one sinner that repenteth."

We must stop regretting that "only ten were converted," and, like the angels, rejoice over one sinner that repenteth.

Then we must turn our thoughts more toward the future, toward the heavenly rest, the heavenly activities and the eternal joys which are there. I repeat, it is a trumpet call. It costs something to have the joy of the Lord. Salvation, with its joy, is a free gift, but the joy of the Lord is to be had only by entering into fellowship with the Lord in His life plan; to be, in the measure of our capacity, Christ's in the world; to get with Him into the joy of suffering; into the joy of the great sweet will of God; into the expectation of the things to come.

It was a great thing for humanity when that strange being, Peter the Hermit, went through Europe preaching the Crusades. It was a call to those barons and knights to cease petty neighborhood wars; to come away from their pompous and empty way of life; from tilting in the castle yard, and feasting in the castle hall, to go forth to do an unselfish thing.

Is not the sorrow and pain of human life a call to a perpetual crusade, a call up out of the petty things in which our lives are frittered away, into sympathy and helpfulness? And is not the sin of the world a call to go out upon Christ's own great enterprise of salvation into the uttermost parts of the earth? It seems to me there is something in this that ought to lay hold of the noble side of us, that ought to redeem us from the meanness of self-pleasing and to lift us up into a glad participation in our Lord's sufferings and also in His unspeakable joy.

VIII

The Consecration

TEXT: "And the priests brought in the ark of the covenant of the Lord unto his place, into the oracle of the house, to the most holy place, even under the wings of the cherubims. For the cherubims spread forth their two wings over the place of the ark, and the cherubims covered the ark and the staves thereof above. And they drew out the staves, that the ends of the staves were seen out in the holy place before the oracle, and they were not seen without; and there they are unto this day. There was nothing in the ark save the two tables of stone, which Moses put there at Horeb, when tne Lord made a covenant with the children of Israel, when they came out of the land of Egypt. And it came to pass, when the priests were come out of the holy place, that the cloud filled the house of the Lord."—1 Kings 8:6-11.

I WISH to begin a study of the subject of Consecration. I believe it to be, in the common apprehension of believers, greatly encumbered with misconceptions. Is consecration God's act or man's act? Is it partly man's act and partly God's act? If so, what is man's part in it?

Beyond doubt the subject is vaguely felt to be important. The religious literature of the time insists upon this importance, and very rarely do Christians come together in conventions, or in any large gathering, without appointing hours for "consecration meetings." And, in fact, there is a great deal of so-called "consecrating" done. The Christian Endeavor societies appoint monthly consecration meetings, and so, in a certain sense, there is a

PERPETUAL CONSECRATION

work going on. There is a great deal of prayer about consecration, and a great deal of talk about it, and a great many directions how to do it, and a great deal of doubt, I believe, at the end, whether it has been done after all— the doubt, of course, growing out of the fact that so many people are continually "reconsecrating" themselves.

Now, is consecration something that requires to be done over and over again? If it is, we ought to know it. We ought to know what degree of frequency there should be in the act of consecration, so that we may be very sure that we keep consecrated all of the time.

I am the more surprised by this confusion,

because God has, so to speak, prepared the subject for our study. He has put into the Bible

TWO GREAT TYPICAL ILLUSTRATIONS

of consecration, one in the consecration of the temple, and the other in the consecration of the priesthood. And you know that both of these types converge upon us, the believers of this dispensation, for we are called both "temples" and "priests."

"For ye are the temple of the living God" (2 Cor. 6:16). "What? know ye not that your body is the temple of the Holy Ghost?" (1 Cor. 6:19). "Ye are a chosen generation, a royal priesthood" (1 Pet. 2:9). "Unto him that loved us, and washed us from our sins in his own blood, and hath made us kings and priests unto God" (Rev. 1:5, 6).

The temple was for the *possession,* the abiding place of God; the priesthood, for the *service* of God; and for each there was an act—consecration. The shekinah did not take possession of the temple until the act of consecration was complete; nor could a priest, though born to the priesthood, enter upon his service until duly consecrated.

My purpose, then, is to study the Temple-type of Consecration.

1. Now, first of all, consider what a wonderful structural analogy there is between that old typical temple, and these living temples which we are.

The temple, as you remember, was in three parts: the court, or outer enclosure, which was public and obvious, and into which any might enter; the holy place, coming next to the court, which was the ordinary place of worship, as the court was of sacrifice; and then, opening out of the holy place, the holy of holies, into which the high priest only—type of Christ, our High Priest—might enter, and which was filled with the glory of the presence of God.

Just so, the living temple is in three parts—the body, outward, obvious and answering to the outer court, in which sacrifice was offered (for remember, Christ "bore our sins in his own body"), the soul, or "heart," the seat of affections, desires, and of the will (and, there-

fore, the sphere of worship, for worship is loving adoration and praise) and, lastly, connected with the soul most intimately in some
way which we do not precisely understand, but
yet distinct from it, the spirit, the highest part
of man, the seat of the reason, the understand-
ing, the imagination—in a word, the mind.
And, just as the body answers to the temple
court, and the soul to the holy place, so the
spirit is, in these living temples, the holy of
holies.

2. Recur now to the passage which is our
text, and which describes the act by which the
temple was consecrated, and we shall see how
the type helps us to understand what our consecration must be if it is to have any real meaning.

I think I am, most of all, struck by the
exceeding simplicity of that act. The priests
simply put the ark of the covenant into the
holy of holies, and then withdrew. God did
the rest.

And the significance of the act is as simple
as the act itself. That ark was, perhaps, the
most important, the most all-inclusive of all

the types of Christ. When God was showing to Moses the patterns in the mount, the first of them all was the ark. In a very real sense, the tabernacle was built around that ark. That ark with its shadowing cherubim and radiant

SHEKINAH GLORY

was the center of Israel's worship and service, and, sprinkled with atoning blood, was Israel's mercy-seat. And, just as the temple was, as to the human side, consecrated when the ark was installed in its inmost apartment, so, when we, by a deliberate, definite act, have surrendered to Him for His exclusive habitation and possession, our whole being, body, soul and spirit, are consecrated.

It is when we come to consider the temple-type in its several parts that we may with certainty know not only how to proceed, but that the act is, indeed, complete. Remember, with the divine part of consecration we have no concern. God may safely be trusted to do His part.

First, then, the priests carried the ark in. God did not send an angel to do that, nor in any way assist by supernatural means. It was an action entirely upon the human side. It was the voluntary, deliberate act of the priests.

Secondly. They carried it into the holy of holies. They did not stop in the court, nor even in the holy place. They kept no part of the temple for themselves. Into its innermost recesses, into that most secret room, made beautiful and costly with gold and precious marbles, and cunning work of the engraver— the very place where pride might most easily entrench itself—they carried the ark.

Thirdly. They drew out the staves. That was an act of exceeding symbolical beauty. You know what the staves were: they were the wooden rods by which the ark was carried from place to place, and there was an express command that during the wilderness wanderings the staves should not be taken out. You see the significance of the action? It was a finality! They did not intend to do that again. They had surrendered the holy of holies to Jehovah for an everlasting possession. Israel had many recurring ceremonials, but "reconsecration" was not one of them. They meant it. It was once for all.

Fourthly. They went out. They did not remain to share the holy of holies with Jehovah. And you observe, it was "when the priests were come out of the holy place, the cloud filled the house of the Lord." I am well persuaded that the cloud would never have filled the house if the priests had remained within. They went out.

Observe, the surrender of the holy of holies was in itself the surrender of the temple. To reach it the ark passed through the court; passed through the holy place. There was no pause,

NO PIECEMEAL SURRENDER,

no separate ceremony for these outer parts of the edifice. To surrender the holy of holies was to surrender the court and the holy place. It is as if some conqueror, taking possession of a surrendered fortress, should pass through the outer defenses, through the inner defenses, and then into the inner citadel and there plant his imperial banner in sign of undisputed occupancy of the whole.

Precisely in this way is consecration presented in the New Testament. "Present your bodies a living sacrifice"—the court. "Let the peace of God rule in your hearts"—the holy place. "Casting down imaginations, and every high thing that exalteth itself against the knowledge of God, and bringing into captivity every thought to the obedience of Christ" —the mind, the holy of holies.

3. Now let us make all of this personal. Perhaps we shall be ready to agree, first of all, that

OUR CONCEPTION OF CONSECRATION

has been poor and inadequate. We have been thinking of service, simply, and that in connection with the body; "take my hands, take my lips, take my feet," and so on, in a kind of sentimental, anatomical way. We have not thought of this temple-type and what it signifies; of being God-filled, God-possessed, quite apart from considerations of service. I grow very weary of the perpetual spurring of

God's dear people to service, service, as if any father ever did care so much to have his children toiling for him, as loving and trusting him. And the more so as the God-possessed Christian invariably does serve. No. There is a higher thought: the enthronement of Jesus as Lord of all.

How is it with us, beloved? Have we, by a definite act of the will, heartily, joyfully, brought Jesus into His own, saying as we passed through the court, "This body, O Lord, is thine; rule it as thou wilt; choose thou its service?" As we passed through the holy place, "Rule thou in my heart, thou Peace of God," and as we came into the spirit: "Here abide, adorable Jesus; subject my reason to the authority of thy word; set my imagination at holy work;

SHINE INTO MY SPIRIT

the radiant glory of thine own, and from this innermost place rule all the temple"?

Then, have we drawn out the staves? You know what that means—it is not to be done over again. I know what you are thinking:

"Perhaps I did not do it well." I dare say
not. The priests may have moved very awk-
wardly; their feelings may not have been what
they ought to have been; their conception of
the meaning of what they were doing may have
been imperfect. But this they did—they took
the ark in and drew out the staves.

And again: When you brought Christ in
did you retire? Or, did you stay in with Him?
Has not that been the trouble?

I remember once hearing a rather excitable
young lady testify in a meeting in New Eng-
land. She said over and over again: "It is
Jesus and I." A dear brother, who sat on the
platform with me, whispered: "I have known
that girl eight or nine years, in fact, I was
her pastor, and that is just the trouble with
her. It is Jesus and the girl. If she can ever
get where she will say: 'It is Jesus only,' she
will have a more even experience."

4. Lastly, one word as to the divine side
of consecration. The priests went out and left
God in possession. It was then that the divine part of consecration was performed, and
not till then. The shekinah of God filled the

house with a glory-cloud which always abode between the wings of the cherubim over the mercy seat, and which spread and increased until all the holy place and the very courts were filled with the radiance. That was God's act.

GOD ACCEPTED THE CONSECRATION

when the priests had put Him where He belonged and when there was no door shut to Him anywhere. There was no shining when He was in the court. There was no shining when He was in holy place, nor even when He was put in the most holy place; nor even when the staves were drawn out; it was not until the priests went out, setting themselves aside, disowning all lordship over the place, and left that building to God that the place was filled with glory. And till that was done, nothing was done.

You know that what the shekinah was to the temple of old, the Holy Spirit is to these temples which we are.

"In whom ye also are builded together for an habitation of God through the Spirit"

(Eph. 2:22). "What? know ye not that your body is the temple of the Holy Ghost which is in you?" (1 Cor. 6:19).

This, then, is the tremendous typical significance of this type of the divine side of consecration—it is the filling of the Holy Spirit. Think of it! The answer of God to the heart-felt, sincere surrender of the whole being to the possession of Jesus Christ is the filling of the whole man, spirit, soul and body; with the Holy Spirit. How insignificant in comparison the human side, and yet how unspeakably important, since the fullness of the Spirit's presence depends upon it.

Friends, we walk by faith, not by sight. The priests of old could see the glory—with which

GOD FILLED THE HOUSE

—we must believe He is there. Ah! just there is the fatal gap with so many. Multitudes in all sincerity surrender the three-fold being to Jesus; and then, because they do not *feel* the Spirit in fuller manifestation, doubt—and repeat the process again and again. Remember, it is not "consecration to service," nor power for service which is before us in the Temple-type; that will be considered when the Priest-type is before us.   It is consecration unto possession.

After all, can anything be simpler than real, biblical consecration.   It is only putting God in His place, giving Him access everywhere, and then going out and leaving Him to the control of that which has been given to Him. Then God will do His part.   He will take possession.

Now, just a few questions.   Have we, as believers, ever definitely brought Jesus into the temple at all?   Have we not regarded Him as an external Master, to whom we gave something which He might use, just as I might take that pencil and write with it?   Have we brought Him within?   Has that been the thought of our consecration?   Have we given Him, by a definite act, the outer court—our bodies?   If we have done that, have we, each one, brought Him into the holy place—our hearts—and said: "Now reign here, reign over me, over my desires and over my affections"?   If we have done that, have we severally brought Him, by a definite act, once for all, into our spirits, and said, "Reign over my reason,

TAKE MY IMAGINATION

and set it to picturing the glories of heaven and the beautiful things of God, and redeem it from the things it is too much occupied with"? And have we said: "Take this intellectual pride of mine, Lord Jesus; I am a poor fool; just come in, and do my thinking for me"?

Then, have we drawn out the staves? Have we said: "Lord, now you are brought in once for all and I draw out the staves; I am not going to do this again next month; I do it now"? And then, having said that, have we not gone out ourselves?

How is it with us? Are we living as if this whole wonderful temple—body, soul and spirit —were no longer ours? It was ours, but we moved out and God moved in, and now it is His. Just when it is that way, I am very sure the glory of God will fill the house.

IX

Defilement and Cleansing

TEXT: "Having therefore these promises, dearly beloved, let us cleanse ourselves from all filthiness of the flesh and spirit, perfecting holiness in the fear of God."—2 Cor. 7:1.

"If we confess our sins, he is faithful and just to forgive us our sins, and to cleanse us from all unrighteousness."—1 John 1:9.

"Peter saith unto him, Thou shalt never wash my feet. Jesus answered him, If I wash thee not, thou hast no part with me."—John 13:8.

WE ARE now to consider Defilement and Cleansing as connected with Consecration. You remember that we have been looking at the subject of consecration, first through the Temple-type; secondly, through the Priest-type. We, as believers, are both temples and priests; and we found in the consecration of the temple for the abiding presence of God, and the consecration of the priests for the service of God, a two-fold type which instructed us concerning our own consecration.

Now, while it is true that neither temple nor priest was ever reconsecrated, it is, alas, true

100

also that both were frequently defiled, and whenever that occurred, cleansing from that defilement was imperative. A defiled priest was still a priest; indeed, he was born a priest, and consecration was but the ceremony which inducted him into his priesthood, into the exercise of its functions, just as coronation puts into rulership one who is born a prince, born with a royal right. We are priests by the new birth, and consecration but opens the door to our service as such. Defilement suspends this privilege of service. A priest defiled was sternly

FORBIDDEN TO SERVE

in the things of God until cleansed, but the method of cleansing was not reconsecration, that was never done again.

Without doubt, it occurred oftentimes, when there was a low spiritual state in Israel, that the priests, who really in God's sight, and according to the Book of God, were defiled, still served at the altar. But nothing could have been more displeasing to God than for them to persist in serving Him with unclean hands;

it was, as we might say, a wanton insult. It was shocking that one of God's priests should be defiled; it was insolent for him, with that defilement upon him, to presume to continue in the service of God. I might quote from the New Testament in this connection to show that God will have no service from a defiled servant. He has made abundant provision for

INSTANT CLEANSING

from defilement, but this He insists upon. "They that bear the vessels of the Lord must have clean hands." I am persuaded that one reason why there is so little fruit from very much of the service of those who unquestionably are God's children, is that they persist in service, or the forms of service, while living upon a low level.

Now I want to take up briefly these two things: defilement and cleansing as connected with consecration.

1. And, first, unpleasant as the matter is, look at defilement. Let us turn in our Bibles to the eighth chapter of Ezekiel. It may be we shall not need to go beyond that chapter,

or, at most, to look at one or two other passages which may serve to bring before our minds the biblical idea of defilement.

"And it came to pass in the sixth year, in the sixth month, in the fifth day of the month, as I sat in mine house, and the elders of Judah sat before me, that the hand of the Lord God fell there upon me. Then I beheld, and lo, a likeness as the appearance of fire: from the appearance of his loins even downward, fire; and from his loins even upward, as the appearance of brightness, as the color of amber. And he put forth the form of a hand, and took me by a lock of mine head; and the spirit lifted me up between the earth and the heaven, and brought me in the

VISIONS OF GOD

to Jerusalem, to the door of the inner gate that looketh toward the north; where was the seat of the image of jealousy, which provoketh to jealousy."

Let me say a word here. This "image of jealousy" was simply an idol. Ezekiel goes in the spirit into the temple, and looking through the gate northward, right toward the altar, he found an idol set up in the very court of that temple, which had once been consecrated to God.

"And, behold, the glory of the God of Israel was there."

That was not the proper place for the glory. The proper place for the shekinah was in the holy of holies over the ark, between the cherubim. We shall see presently why the glory had withdrawn from the holy of holies of the temple, and was abiding there; probably invisible to the eyes of apostate Israel, but visible to the faithful prophet.

"Then said he unto me, Son of man, lift up thine eyes now the way toward the north. So I lifted up mine eyes the way toward the north, and behold northward at the gate of the altar, this

IMAGE OF JEALOUSY

in the entry. He said furthermore unto me, Son of man, seest thou what they do? even the great abominations that the house of Israel

committeth here, that I should go far off from
my sanctuary?"

God, as it were, had withdrawn from the
inner room, from the place of His enthronement, but still standing by the altar that spake
of sacrifice. The higher blessings withdrawn,
there was still the brazen altar for a point of
meeting with God. Justification remains,
blessed be God, even when His people have no
heart for holiness.

"But turn thee yet again, and thou shalt
see greater abominations. And he brought
me to the door of the court; and when I looked,
behold a hole in the wall. Then said he unto
me, Son of man, dig now in the wall: and when
I had digged in the wall, behold a door. And
he said unto me, Go in, and behold the wicked
abominations that they do here. So I went
in and saw; and behold every form of creep-
ing things, and abominable beasts, and all the
idols of the house of Israel, portrayed upon
the wall round about."

There was defilement with a vengeance.
They were not going in by the usual way
through the veil; they had made themselves

A SECRET WAY

into the holy of holies. They had actually gone into the inner abiding place of God, which He had taken possession of at the consecration of that temple by the shining cloud of His glory, and had painted those golden walls with all the abominations of lust and idolatry!

"And there stood before them seventy men of the ancients of the house of Israel, and in the midst of them stood Jaazaniah the son of Shaphan, with every man his censer in his hand; and a thick cloud of incense went up."

They had dispossessed God, so to speak, from the holy of holies, and there they had pictured their idols, which were too filthy and obscene for the world to see. And, in secret, getting in by a hole in the wall, they were offering incense to those unspeakable things. Out in the outer court, where every one could see, the priests were still going through the form of the regular ritual of Israel; the lamb smoking on the altar every morning and every night, and by it stood the priest in the sacred garments of priesthood! And there, just there, invisible to the defiled eyes of His priest, awful in His nearness, was the God of the altar —cast out of the holy of holies, which was painted with abominations.

"Then said he unto me, Son of man, hast thou seen what the ancients of the house of Israel do in the dark, every man in the chambers of his imagery?"

Surely, exposition is not needed here. In the court an idol. Within the holy place an idol. Within the holy of holies,

ALL CONCEALED

from the eyes of man, unspeakable abominations upon the painted walls, and the elders of Israel secretly offering incense.

But apply the type. We are, in ourselves, that which corresponds to the temple, the court, the holy place, and the holy of holies—the body, the heart, the mind. Do we know something of all this? Putting Jesus, by the act of consecration, into possession of the whole being, enshrining Him in heart and mind— and then letting loose the imagination to paint the walls of that inner chamber with pictures

we would not wish the world to see? And
do we like to go in there to see all this while
keeping up our church-going — perhaps
preaching or teaching Sunday-school classes—
living before the world in the profession of being God's people? Do we know anything about
that? Or, if that be not our case, are we putting *some* idol into the temple,

SOME DARLING THING

that comes between us and God, while all the
time our lips are saying: "Yes, God is supreme"; do we know anything of that? It
may be money, or social position, or a habit, or
just self—the ugliest idol of all.

"Then said he unto me, Son of man, hast
thou seen what the ancients of the house of
Israel do in the dark, every man in the chamber of his imagery?"

All this was in the dark. I wonder if we
would be willing to have the pictures which
our imagination paints taken right out and
shown to our fellowmen!

"He said also unto me, Turn thee yet again,
and thou shalt see greater abominations than

they do. Then he brought me to the door of the gate of the Lord's house which was toward the north; and, behold, there sat women weeping for Tammuz."

Tammuz—sun-god worship. When the sun went down, they worshipped him by weeping, as if he had died. And every morning they greeted the sun as if he were born again. That was pretty bad for the temple of Jehovah, was it not?

"Then said he unto me, Hast thou seen this, O son of man? turn thee yet again, and thou shalt

SEE GREATER ABOMINATIONS

than these. And he brought me into the inner court of the Lord's house, and, behold, at the door of the temple of the Lord, between the porch and the altar, were about five and twenty men, with their backs toward the temple of the Lord, and their faces toward the east; and they worshipped the sun toward the east."

Now sun worship, in the very essence of it, is simply nature worship. The sun is the most glorious object which meets the eye as we look

abroad upon nature.   It is that on which life
and comfort and all those things depend, and
naturally, therefore, to the heart that has gone
away from God, a kind of center of that worship which goes out toward the powers of nature.

You may say that I am wasting time to
dwell upon this, that we have nothing like sun
worship in this country, nothing like turning
our backs to the altar of God, and worshipping
the sun.   I beg your pardon, we have.   This
is precisely

THE MOST SUBTLE ABOMINATION

permitted today in the thoughts and hearts of
Christian people.   It finds expression in the
extraordinary deference of the modern church
to so-called science.   Multitudes are turning
away from the Bible accounts of creation, and
of the origin of man, to the improved theories
and plausible hypotheses of alleged scientists;
theories which hide God behind phenomena,
and deny the supernatural.   Witness the pur-
chase by professed Christians of thousands
upon thousands of volumes of "Natural Law

in the Spiritual World." Witness the importation by professed Christians of Henry Drummond to lecture upon the "Ascent of Man," while they know that their Bibles give one long testimony to the descent of man. Never perhaps in all the history of the church was there such a turning of the back upon the altar of God and the temple of God to worship nature, as now, and never were these things doing such serious harm.   To millions of professed Christians Drummond and Darwin are more authoritative than Moses.

Now to sum up for a moment these defilements: The idol in the holy place; the

INNER CHAMBER PAINTED

with all manner of vileness, and the elders of Israel loving to be there, while out in the court men turn their backs upon the altar of God, too "advanced" to endure a dripping cross, and esthetically worship the sun.

Turn now to the New Testament:

"And the Jews' passover was at hand, and Jesus went up to Jerusalem, and found in the temple those that sold oxen and sheep and

doves, and the changers of money sitting: and
when he had made a scourge of small cords,
he drove them all out of the temple, and the
sheep, and the oxen; and poured out the changers' money, and overthrew the tables; and said
unto them that sold doves, Take these things
hence; make not my Father's house an house
of merchandise" (John 2:13-16).

Perhaps, we are beginning to apply the doc-
trine of this passage to the temples of brick
and stone and wood which we have erected for
the worship of God; but the deeper truth always lies back of the symbol, and we have here
the thought illustrated for us of the prostitu-
tion of the natural powers of man to the mere
pursuit of gain; the taking of the body and
making

A MONEY-MAKING MACHINE

out of it, or an eating and drinking machine,
nothing else; that body, which is the temple of
God. Do we know anything of this?

Without going further, we have here cer-
tainly that which ought to search us. We have
the thought of idols coming in between our-

selves and God, and claiming our affections, also the thought of the mind polluted, the imagination suffered to wander into things that are unclean and painting the inner chambers with foul imagery kept very secret; of turning the back upon the altar of God in mad worship of nature and nature's laws.

2. Let us turn now to the provision, alike sublime, simple and adequate, which God has made for our cleansing.

First of all, let us look for a moment at one of the most familiar passages in the word of God.

"If we confess our sins, he is faithful and just to forgive us our sins, and to cleanse us from all unrighteousness" (1 John 1:9).

There is something then for us to do in the matter of cleansing when we have become defiled.

"If we confess our sins." That is a very different thing, and far more searching in its import than the mere confession of sinfulness. We do that very readily. There is not one of us but what would say: "Yes, I am a sinner."

"If we confess our *sins.*" That means just taking the hateful things up one by one and showing them to God, saying: "I did this, and that, and that." Every parent has observed that it is very easy to get a general confession from children that they have been disobedient, but it is not so easy to get them to tell just *what* they have been doing that is wrong.

Confessing our sins is taking a hateful sin and holding it up before God, and letting Him look at it. Held up before God, in that white light, a sin does not look nearly so pretty as it did when we yielded to the temptation.

That is the human side of cleansing—confession. I need not say that this is a believer's privilege. The Christ-rejecter might confess his sins until he fell into perdition, and his sins would be just the same as before. "No man cometh unto the Father, but by me," says Christ. There is but one way of salvation—the way of faith. But when we who have believed have confessed our sins then we may claim the promise:

"He is faithful and just to forgive us our

sins, and to cleanse us from all unrighteousness." First, forgiveness; then cleansing.

How simple this is! Now connect it with the third text I gave you: Peter saying "Thou shalt never wash my feet," and Christ saying: "If I wash thee not, thou hast no part with me." You see, there is no other resource. When we have become defiled we must

RUN AWAY TO JESUS

and humbly put the defiled feet in His pierced hand. But when that has been done faith says: "Now I am cleansed."

The Christian who has confessed his sins ought not to go about with a sense of the divine displeasure, nor with the sense of defilement. Faith says: "I have done that which God requires from me, and now I believe He is indeed faithful, and has done His part of it. He has forgiven me, and there is no frown on His blessed face. He has cleansed me, and I am clean, and am going forward in His service with the full assurance that He is abiding sweetly once more in the very secret chambers of my being."

We must, as in salvation, take the divine part of it by faith.

As in consecration we yield ourselves for it and then believe we are consecrated because we dare not doubt that God does His part, so, when that consecration has become defiled, we confess the thing in all its detail to God, and we go away happy because we believe God has again done His part—has forgiven us, has cleansed us.

After all, it is all by faith. We begin by faith and we go on by faith. That which is required of us is simple and reasonable and we do it, and then we believe God has done that which He promised he would do.

After all, how very simple it is! I may have made it very difficult, although it was in my heart to make it exceedingly simple. First of all,

THE YIELDING TO GOD

for consecration, followed by a definite act of faith which says: "God has done it; I am consecrated." Then when defilement comes in, confession, and then again the act of faith, which says: "God has cleansed me, and once more I am clean every whit." Then we go forward in His service expecting the manifestation of His glorious power, and then His peace garrisons our hearts and minds through Christ Jesus.